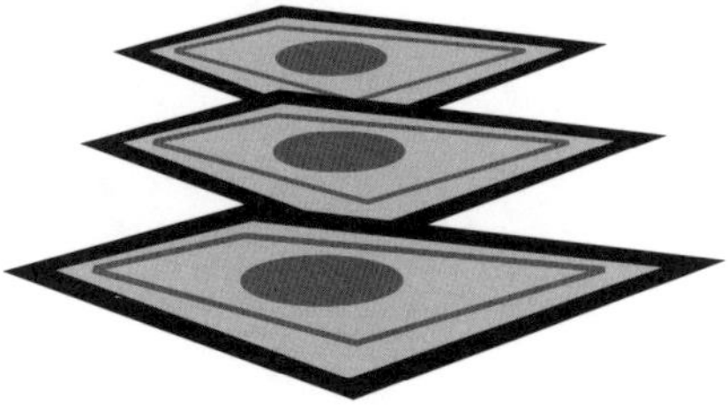

Money Quotes

Money Quotes

300

Sayings

and

Poems

leonard roy frank

Gramercy Books
New York

Previously published as *Money: The Greatest Things Ever Said.*

This 2005 edition is published by Gramercy Books, an imprint of Random House Value Publishing, by arrangement with Random House Reference, divisions of Random House, Inc., New York.

Random House
New York • Toronto • London • Sydney • Auckland
www.randomhouse.com

Printed and bound in China.

A catalog record for this title is available from the Library of Congress.

ISBN 0-517-22548-4

10 9 8 7 6 5 4 3 2 1

INTRODUCTION

What is there about money that we humans find so fascinating? It's the spur of youth, the balm of age, the measure of one's ability to command the services of others, economic power quantified. The amount we have of it greatly influences our standing in the community and, for many, the way we feel about ourselves. Only a fool would "underestimate the power of cash." Indeed, money is power; if you don't believe it, try filling your gas tank with an empty wallet. On the other hand, it may be even more foolhardy to overestimate the power of money for, as almost everyone knows, money can't buy happiness, love, or peace of mind. Yes, although money may work wonders, it has never produced any miracles.

This book contains more than 275 quotations about money—some instructive, some entertaining; some familiar, some unfamiliar; some wise, some otherwise. My intention is not so much to promote a particular point of view as to present a wide-ranging assortment of ideas that will stimulate readers to think about the place of money in their lives, what it is now and what it might be in the future were attitudes and circumstances to change.

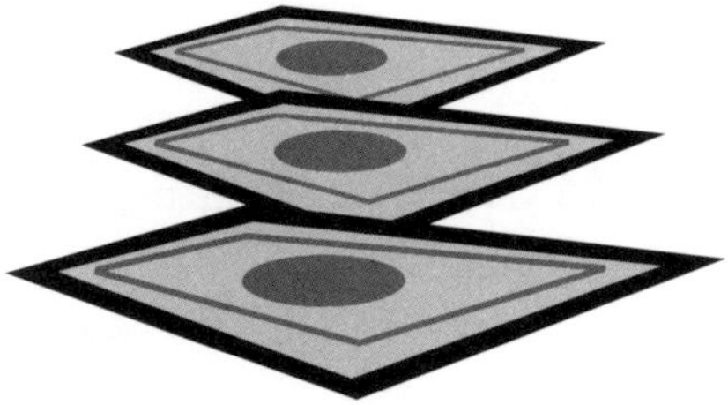

Money Quotes

A BILLION HERE, a billion there, and pretty soon you're talking about real money.

Everett Dirksen, Illinois senator, 1896–1969

Money is the sinews of love as well as war.

George Farquhar, Irish playwright, 1677–1707

Wealth is not without its advantages and the case to the contrary, although it has often been made, has never proved widely persuasive.

John Kenneth Galbraith, contemporary Canadian-born U.S. economist

MONEY, it turned out, was exactly like sex, you thought of nothing else if you didn't have it and thought of other things if you did.

James Baldwin, U.S. writer, 1924–1987

Money is like sex; only too much is enough.

John Updike, contemporary U.S. writer

WEALTH IS NOT his who has it, but his who enjoys it.

English Proverb

HOLDUP MAN: Your money or your life? Come on, hurry up!
BENNY: I'm thinking it over!

Jack Benny, U.S. comedian, 1894–1974

When a fellow says, "It ain't the money, but the principle of the thing," *it's the money.*

Kin Hubbard, U.S. journalist and humorist, 1868–1930

MONEY is the sixth sense which enables you to enjoy the other five.

W. Somerset Maugham, English writer, 1874–1965

I have a sixth sense, but not the other five. If I wasn't making money, they'd put me away.

Red Skelton, U.S. entertainer, 1913–1997

Money is the sincerest form of flattery.
Leonard Roy Frank, contemporary U.S. editor

Money has only one use—to give us independence from our enemies.
Humphrey Bogart, U.S. actor, 1899–1957

Money couldn't buy friends but it got you a better class of enemy.
Spike Milligan, Irish entertainer and writer, 1918–2002

WITH money in your pocket, you are wise, you are handsome, and you sing well too.

Yiddish Proverb

Money is honey—my little sonny!
And a rich man's joke is always funny.

T. E. Brown, English poet, 1830–1897

A man who knows how to make good bargains or finds his money increase in his coffers thinks presently that he has a good deal of brains and is almost fit to be a statesman.

Jean de La Bruyère, French moralist, 1645–1696

Nothing so gives the illusion of intelligence as personal association with large sums of money.

John Kenneth Galbraith, contemporary

THAT is the use of money: it enables us to get what we want instead of what other people think we want.

George Bernard Shaw, English playwright, 1856–1950

Money is the only substance which can keep a cold world from nicknaming a citizen "Hey, you!"

Wilson Mizner, U.S. screenwriter and humorist, 1876–1933

WHEN THE HISTORY of guilt is written, parents who refuse their children money will be right up there in the Top Ten.

Erma Bombeck, U.S. writer and humorist, 1927–1996

Like that of words and feelings, money's value is impalpable. Yet money lasts, it doesn't flit by. Nor does it ask anything of its possessor. It melts, like ice cream, but very slowly, in the warmth of inflation. It has endurance and extension. These little disks and shallow sculptures enlist us in a conspiracy of users; a penny from a child's hand is worth just what it is from a grownup's. Getting and spending confer an instant dignity.

John Updike, contemporary U.S. writer

The women who do the most work get the least money, and the women who have the most money do the least work.

Charlotte Perkins Gilman, U.S. writer and lecturer, 1860–1935

Woman's ability to earn money is a better protection against the tyranny and brutality of man than her ability to vote.

Victoria Claflin Woodhull, U.S. women's rights activist and writer, 1838–1927

MONEY MAKES THE MAN.

Greek Proverb

Money makes a man laugh.

John Selden, English historian, 1584–1654

Money makes the mare go.

English Proverb

MONEY MAKES THE WORLD GO ROUND.

U.S. Proverb

Money makes the pot boil though the devil spit in the fire.

English Proverb

Money makes friends enemies.

English Proverb

MONEY IS COINED LIBERTY.

Fyodor Dostoyevsky, Russian writer, 1821–1881

Wealth may be an excellent thing, for it means power, it means leisure, it means liberty.

James Russell Lowell, U.S. poet, 1819–1991

The price we have to pay for money is paid in liberty.

Robert Louis Stevenson, Scottish writer, 1850–1894

Riches mean freedom from niggling details.

James David Barber, contemporary U.S. political scientist

It is pretty to see what money will do.

Samuel Pepys, English government official and diarist, 1633–1703

Never underestimate the power of cash.

Georgia-Pacific Corp., ad headline, 1990

CASH IS VIRTUE.

Lord Byron, English poet, 1788–1824

Money buys access; access buys influence.

Elizabeth Drew, contemporary U.S. journalist (referring to campaign contributions, 1997)

Money gave me exactly what I wanted, power over others.

Oscar Wilde, English playwright, 1854–1900

As wealth is power, so all power will infallibly draw wealth to itself by some means or other.

Edmund Burke, English statesman, 1729–1797

Money to get power, power to protect money.

Medici, Italian family, fifteenth century (motto)

Follow the money!

Edward Bennett Williams, U.S. lawyer, 1920–1988 (attributed; the watchword for investigative reporters popularized in the film All the President's Men, *1976)*

SHOW ME THE MONEY!

Cameron Crowe, contemporary U.S. screenwriter and director (in the film Jerry Maguire, *1997)*

INTERVIEWER: What's the secret of your lasting success in show business?
YOUNGMAN: Don't believe all the baloney people tell you when they're describing what they're going to do for you someday soon. Get the money!

Henny Youngman, U.S. comedian, 1906–1998

WEALTH is a power usurped by the few to compel the many to labor for their benefit.

Percy Bysshe Shelley, English poet, 1792–1822

MONEY IS GOD'S LIEUTENANT.

Spanish Proverb

Money is the God of this world.

English Proverb

Whoever controls the volume of money in any country is absolute master of all industry and commerce.

James Garfield, U.S. president, 1831–1881

On Wall Street he and a few others—how many?—three hundred, four hundred, five hundred?—had become precisely that...Masters of the Universe. There was...no limit whatsoever.

Tom Wolfe, contemporary U.S. writer

THE ALMIGHTY DOLLAR, that great object of universal devotion throughout our land.

Washington Irving, U.S. writer, 1783–1859

Money is the alienated essence of man's work and existence; this essence dominates him and he worships it.

Karl Marx, German economist, 1818–1883

When it is a question of money, everybody is of the same religion.

Voltaire, French philosopher, 1604–1778

I'm a millionaire. That is my religion.

George Bernard Shaw, British playwright, 1856–1950

I believe the power to make money is a gift of God.

John D. Rockefeller Sr., U.S. industrialist, 1839–1937

**Some people's money is merited
And other people's is inherited.**

Ogden Nash, U.S. writer and poet, 1902–1971

UNTIL THE AGE of twelve I sincerely believed that everybody had a house on Fifth Avenue, a villa in Newport and a steam-driven, ocean-going yacht.

Cornelius Vanderbilt Jr., U.S. railroad magnate, 1843–1899

At the bottom, people tend to believe that class is defined by the amount of money you have. In the middle, people grant that money has something to do with it, but think education and the kind of work you do almost equally important. Nearer the top, people perceive that taste, values, ideas, style, and behavior are indispensable criteria of class, *regardless of money or occupation or education.*

Paul Fussell, contemporary U.S. academic and writer

The great rule is not to talk about money with people who have much more or much less than you.

Katharine Whitehorn, contemporary English writer

Money is paper blood.

Bob Hope, contemporary English-born U.S. entertainer

MONEY IS THE ACE OF TRUMPS.

English Proverb

MONEY is the mother's milk of politics.

Jesse Unruh, U.S. political leader, 1922–1983

Money is the crack cocaine of politics.

Jim Hightower, contemporary U.S. journalist

MONEY-MAKING is our magician's serpent, remaining today sole master of the field. The best class we show, is but a mob of fashionably dressed speculators and vulgarians.

Walt Whitman, U.S. poet, 1819–1891

Having money is just the best thing in the world.

Madonna, contemporary U.S. singer and actor

Money is not required to buy one necessity of the soul.

Henry David Thoreau, U.S. philosopher, 1817–1862

MONEY always implies the promise of magic, but the effect is much magnified when, as now, people have lost faith in everything else.

Lewis H. Lapham, contemporary U.S. writer and editor

Ready money is Aladdin's lamp.

Lord Byron, English poet, 1788–1824

Lord Fermor: Young people, nowadays, imagine that money is everything.
Lord Henry: Yes, and when they grow older they know it.

Oscar Wilde, English playwright, 1854–1900 (in the play The Picture of Dorian Gray, *1891)*

Money isn't everything, but it's a long way ahead of what comes next.

Sir Edmund Stockdale, contemporary-century London mayor

There are more important things than money—the only trouble is they all cost money.

Louis A. Safian, contemporary U.S. writer

Elizabeth Taylor: Money isn't all, Jed.
James Dean: Not when you got it.

Edna Ferber, U.S. writer, 1887–1968 (in the film Giant, *1956)*

NEVER WORK JUST for money or for power. They won't save your soul or help you sleep at night.

Marian Wright Edelman, contemporary U.S. lawyer and children's rights leader

Money will buy a pretty good dog, but it won't buy the wag of his tail.

Josh Billings, U.S. writer and humorist, 1818–1885

"Money does not bring happiness"—only the wherewithal, perhaps, *to endure its absence.*

Barbara Ehrenreich, contemporary U.S. writer

MONEY can't buy everything; for example, poverty.

Nelson Algren, U.S. writer, 1909–1981

Riches may not bring happiness, but neither does poverty.

Sophie Irene Loeb, Russian-born U.S. journalist, 1874–1929

WHAT'S THE USE of happiness? It can't buy you money.

Henny Youngman, U.S. comedian, 1906–1998

Those who think money can do anything are likely to do anything for money.

English Proverb

If I'd have known what having it all was going to be like, I'd have *settled for less.*

Jane Wagner, contemporary U.S. writer

I DON'T care too much for money,
For money can't buy me love.

John Lennon and Paul McCartney, contemporary English songwriters and singers

Who marries for money earns it.

Proverb

I DON'T LIKE money, actually, but it quiets my nerves.

Joe Louis, U.S. prizefighter, 1914–1981

I can remember way back when a liberal was someone who was generous with his own money.

Will Rogers, U.S. writer, actor, and humorist, 1879–1935

Nowadays people know the price of everything and the value of nothing.

Oscar Wilde, English playwright, 1854–1900

Health without money is half-sickness.

English Proverb

The first wealth is health.

Ralph Waldo Emerson, U.S. philosopher, 1803–1882

Better health without wealth than wealth without health.

Proverb

MANY people despise money, but few hurry to give it away.

François de La Rochefoucauld, French writer, 1613–1680

Money is one burden everyone is willing to bear.

English Proverb

No client ever had enough to bribe my conscience or to stop its utterance against wrong and oppression.

Abraham Lincoln, U.S. president, 1809–1865 (attributed)

It is no light thing to have secured a livelihood on condition of going through life masked and gagged.

John Morley, English writer, 1838–1923

It is difficult to get a man to understand something when his salary depends upon his not understanding it.

Upton Sinclair, U.S. writer, 1878–1968

MONEY often costs too much.

Ralph Waldo Emerson, U.S. philosopher, 1803–1882

The cost of a thing is the amount of life it requires to be exchanged for it, immediately or in the long run.

Henry David Thoreau, U.S. philosopher, 1817–1862

MONEY TALKS.

English Proverb

Money doesn't talk, it swears.

Bob Dylan, contemporary U.S. songwriter and singer

They say "Money talks." All it ever said to me was **"GOOD–BYE."**

Cary Grant, English-born U.S. actor, 1904–1986

When money talks, there are few interruptions.

Herbert V. Prochnow, U.S. economist, banker, and government official, 1897–1998

Not only does money speak; it also imposes silence.

Aldous Huxley, English writer, 1894–1963

IF YOU'D KNOW the value of money, go and borrow some.

Benjamin Franklin, U.S. printer, inventor, and statesman, 1706–1790

Who recalls when folks got along without something if it cost too much?

Kin Hubbard, U.S. journalist and humorist, 1868–1930

We all run in debt for things we wouldn't think of paying perfectly good money for.

Kin Hubbard, U.S. journalist and humorist, 1868–1930

It's not politics that is worrying this country; it's the second payment.

Will Rogers, U.S. writer, actor, and humorist, 1879–1935

If you think nobody cares whether you're alive or not, try missing a couple of car payments.

Earl Wilson, U.S. journalist, 1907–1987

LET US all be happy and live within our means, even if we have to borrow the money to do it with.

Artemus Ward, U.S. writer, lecturer, and humorist, 1834–1867

Creditors have better memories than debtors.

English Proverb

Expenditure rises to meet income.

C. Northcote Parkinson, English political scientist, 1909–1993
(Parkinson's Law)

MONEY DOESN'T GROW ON TREES.

U.S. Proverb

Money is a good servant but a bad master.

French Proverb

An ass is but an ass though laden with gold.

English Proverb

A FOOL and his money are soon parted.

English Proverb

There was a time when a fool and his money were soon parted, but now it happens to everybody.

Adlai E. Stevenson, Illinois governor, presidential candidate, and UN ambassador, 1900–1965

A fool and his money are soon partying.

Anonymous

The Golden Rule: whoever has the gold makes the rules.

Anonymous

A golden key opens every door except that of heaven.

Danish Proverb

Chains of gold, still a slave.

English Proverb

THERE ARE FEW WAYS in which a man can be more innocently employed than in getting money.

Samuel Johnson, English writer and lexicographer, 1709–1784

Money is like promises, easier made than kept.

Josh Billings, U.S. writer and humorist, 1818–1885

MONEY BEGETS MONEY.

Italian Proverb

MONEY, says the proverb, makes money. When you have got a little, it is often easy to get more. The great difficulty is to get that little.

Adam Smith, Scottish economist and philosopher, 1723–1790

Most people are too busy earning a living to make any money.

Anonymous

The most valuable of all human possessions, next to a superior and disdainful air, is the reputation of being well-to-do.

H. L. Mencken, U.S. journalist, 1880–1956

THE shortest and best way of making your fortune is to let people clearly see that it is in their interest to promote yours.

Jean de La Bruyère, French moralist, 1645–1696

Always try to rub up against money, for if you rub up against money long enough, some of it may rub off on you.

Damon Runyon, U.S. journalist, 1884–1946

THE ART OF becoming "rich" is not absolutely nor finally the art of accumulating much money for ourselves, but also of contriving that our neighbors shall have less. In accurate terms, it is "the art of establishing the maximum inequality in our own favor."

John Ruskin, English art critic and writer, 1819–1900

The best way to attract money, she had discovered, was to give the appearance of *having it.*

Gail Sheehy, contemporary U.S. writer

Much industry and little conscience make a man rich.

English Proverb

Not even a collapsing world looks dark to a man who is about to make his fortune.

E. B. White, U.S. writer, 1899–1985

When a man tells you that he got rich through hard work, ask him: **"WHOSE?"**

Don Marquis, U.S. writer and humorist, 1878–1937

The easiest way to make a small fortune is to start with a large one.

Anonymous

Energy makes more fortunes than prudence.

Marquis de Vauvenargues, French soldier and moralist, 1715–1747

MONEY doesn't bring courage, I learned. It's the other way around. Once I took that lesson to heart, I began to rebuild my life.

Suze Orman, contemporary U.S. writer and financial adviser

A man complained that on his way home to dinner he had every day to pass through that long field of his neighbor's. I advised him to buy it, and it would never seem long again.

Ralph Waldo Emerson, U.S. philosopher, 1803–1882

Money was never a big motivation for me, except as a way to keep score. The real excitement is playing the game.

Donald J. Trump, contemporary U.S. real estate investor

The way to wealth, if you desire it, is as plain as the way to market. It depends chiefly on two words, industry and frugality.

Benjamin Franklin, U.S. printer, inventor, and statesman, 1706–1790

The art of getting rich consists not in industry, much less in saving, but in a better order, a timeliness, in being at the right spot.

Ralph Waldo Emerson, U.S. philosopher, 1803–1882

A penny in a pinch is worth a pound.

English Proverb

A penny saved is a penny earned.

English Proverb

Penny wise, pound foolish.

English Proverb

TAKE CARE OF THE PENNIES and the pounds will take care of themselves.

English Proverb

WATCH the costs and the profits will take care of themselves.

Andrew Carnegie, Scottish-born U.S. industrialist, 1835–1919

Beware of little expenses. A small leak will sink a great ship.

Benjamin Franklin, U.S. printer, inventor, and statesman, 1706–1790

Avarice is the spur of industry.

David Hume, English philosopher, 1711–1776

Greed for ownership has taken such a hold of us that we seem to be possessed by wealth rather than to possess it.

Pliny the Younger, Roman writer, first century A.D.

We have extravagance and greed, public poverty and private opulence.

Cato the Younger, Roman statesman, first century B.C.

Epidemic greed is a symptom not of reveling in present triumphs but of a fear that the game is winding down.

Laurence Shames, contemporary U.S. writer

Anonymous: How much money is enough?

Rockefeller: A little more.

John D. Rockefeller Sr., U.S. industrialist, 1839–1937

MUCH WOULD HAVE MORE.

English Proverb

If all the rich men in the world divided up their money among themselves, there wouldn't be enough to go round.

Christina Stead, Australian writer, 1902–1983

Many have by far too much,
but nobody has enough.

Vermont Proverb

THERE are plenty of good five-cent cigars in the country. The trouble is they cost a quarter. What the country really needs is a good five-cent nickel.

Franklin P. Adams, U.S. writer, 1881–1960

I've got all the money I'll ever need, if I die by four o'clock.

Henny Youngman, U.S. comedian, 1906–1998

NEVER IN THE FIELD of economics have so few been given so much at the expense of so many.

Hillary Rodham Clinton, contemporary U.S. first lady and New York senator (referring to President George W. Bush's tax-reduction proposals, January 2003)

The subjects of every state ought to contribute towards the support of the government, as nearly as possible, in proportion to their respective abilities; that is, in proportion to the revenue which they respectively enjoy under the protection of the state.

Adam Smith, Scottish economist and philosopher, 1723–1790

There is no art which one government sooner learns from another than that of draining money from the pockets of the people.

Adam Smith, Scottish economist and philosopher, 1723–1790

The art of government consists in taking as much money as possible from one class of citizens and giving it to the other.

Voltaire, French writer, 1694–1778

THE ONLY THING that hurts more than having to pay an income tax is not having an income to tax.

Anonymous (U.S.)

The taxpayer—that's someone who works for the federal government but doesn't have to take a civil service examination.

Ronald Reagan, contemporary U.S. president

SUGGESTED SIMPLIFIED TAX FORM: How much money did you make last year? Mail it in.

Stanton Delaplane, U.S. journalist, 1907–1988

FUNNY, every time I make out my income tax, I find myself humming, "All of me, why not take all of me?"

Tom Wilson, contemporary U.S. cartoonist

I believe we should all pay our tax bill with a smile. I tried—but they wanted cash.

Anonymous (U.S.)

What is the difference between a taxidermist and a tax collector? The taxidermist takes only your skin.

Mark Twain, U.S. writer and humorist, 1835–1910

The income tax has made more liars out of the American people than golf has.

Will Rogers, U.S. writer, actor, and humorist, 1879–1935

NOBODY ever bet enough on the winning horse.

Anonymous (U.S.)

The less you bet, the more you lose when you win.

Anonymous (U.S.)

FINANCIAL GENIUS consists almost entirely of avarice and a rising market.

John Kenneth Galbraith, contemporary Canadian-born U.S. economist

Insider information is the coin of the realm.

James Stewart, contemporary U.S. journalist (referring to the stock market)

The only absolutely safe way to double your money is to fold it once and put it in your hip pocket.

Kin Hubbard, U.S. journalist and humorist, 1868–1930

IN financial-market history, when people of modest means become swept up in the speculation, it usually means that a climax is approaching.

William Greider, contemporary U.S. journalist

The suckers haven't permanently deserted the stock market. They are merely waiting until the prices get too high again.

Will Rogers, U.S. writer, actor, and humorist, 1879–1935 (attributed)

HOW DO WE KNOW when irrational exuberance has unduly escalated [stock market] values, which then become subject to unexpected and prolonged contractions as they have in Japan over the last decade?

Alan Greenspan, contemporary U.S. Federal Reserve Board chairman, December 1996

The oldest rule in economics, for which I take credit, is that when someone says we have entered a new era of permanent prosperity, *you should take cover.*

John Kenneth Galbraith, contemporary Canadian-born U.S. economist

October. This is one of the peculiarly dangerous months to speculate in stocks. The others are, July, January, September, April, November, May, March, June, December, August, and February.

Mark Twain, U.S. writer and humorist, 1835–1910

The stock market is a pendulum swinging between fear and greed.

Richard Teitelbaum, contemporary U.S. journalist

Buy straw hats in the wintertime. Summer will surely come.

Bernard Baruch, U.S. financier, 1870–1965

BUY LOW, SELL HIGH.

Wall Street Proverb

Never throw good money after bad.

Wall Street Proverb

Stock prices fall faster than they rise.

Wall Street Proverb

No one was ever ruined by taking a profit.

Wall Street Proverb

’TIS the part of a wise man to keep himself today for tomorrow, and not venture all his eggs in one basket.

Miguel de Cervantes, Spanish writer, 1547–1616

Put all your eggs in the one basket and—watch that basket.

Mark Twain, U.S. writer and humorist, 1835–1910

IT'S JUST AS I have been constantly telling you, "Don't gamble"; take all your savings and buy some good stock and hold it till it goes up, then sell it. If it don't go up, don't buy it.

Will Rogers, U.S. writer, actor, and humorist, 1879–1935 (tongue-in-cheek advice offered a few days after the stock-market crash of 1929)

More people get killed chasing after a higher yield than looking down the barrel of a gun.

William LeFevre, contemporary U.S. investment analyst

RULE NO. 1: Never lose money. **RULE NO. 2:** Never forget Rule No. 1.

Warren Buffett, contemporary U.S. financier

Question: "Why do you rob banks?"
Sutton: Because that's where the money is.

Willie Sutton, U.S. bank robber, 1901–1980

A bank is a place where they lend you an umbrella in fair weather and ***ask for it back when it begins to rain.***

Robert Frost, U.S. poet, 1873–1963

Private banking: the process by which banks redistribute the national income, among themselves.

Leo Rosten, U.S. writer, 1908–1997

WHERE LARGE SUMS of money are concerned, it is advisable to trust nobody.

Agatha Christie, English writer, 1891–1975

One can never be too thin or too rich.

Duchess of Windsor (Wallis Simpson Warfield), U.S. society figure, 1896–1986

There is a gigantic difference between earning a great deal of money and being rich.

Marlene Dietrich, German-born U.S. actor, 1901–1992

IF YOU CAN actually count your money, then you are not really rich.

J. Paul Getty, U.S. industrialist, 1892–1976

There are a handful of people whom money won't spoil, and we all count ourselves among them.

Mignon McLaughlin, contemporary U.S. writer and humorist

Get money. Get it quickly. Get it in abundance. Get it in prodigious abundance. Get it dishonestly if you can, honestly if you must.

Mark Twain, U.S. writer and humorist, 1835–1910

WE SIMPLY MUST BELIEVE that the American rich are happy, else our confidence in the whole endeavor might be shaken. For of all the possible values of human society, one and one only is the truly sovereign, truly universal, truly sound, truly and completely acceptable goal of man in America. That goal is money, and let there be no sour grapes about it from the losers.

C. Wright Mills, U.S. sociologist, 1916–1962

There is nothing so characteristic of narrowness and littleness of soul as the love of riches.

Cicero, Roman statesman, first century B.C.

IT is a reproach to religion and government to suffer so much poverty and excess.

William Penn, English Quaker leader and governor of Pennsylvania, 1644–1718

Money never goes to jail.

Arab Proverb

It seems to be a law in American life that whatever enriches us anywhere except in the wallet inevitably becomes uneconomic.

Russell Baker, contemporary U.S. journalist

I'd ask around 10 or 15 people for suggestions. Finally one lady friend asked the right question. "Well, what do you love most?" That's how I started painting money.

Andy Warhol, U.S. artist, 1927–1987

THE love of money is the root of all evil.

Paul, Hebrew Christian apostle, first century A.D. (1 Timothy 6:10)

Lack of money is the root of all evil.

George Bernard Shaw, British playwright, 1856–1950

GREAT WEALTH always supports the party in power, no matter how corrupt it may be. It never exerts itself for reform, for it instinctively fears change. It never struggles against misgovernment. When threatened by the holders of political power, it does not agitate, nor appeal to the public; it buys them off.

Henry George, U.S. economist, 1839–1897

THE RICH MAN IS ALWAYS SOLD TO THE INSTITUTION WHICH MAKES HIM RICH.

Henry David Thoreau, U.S. philosopher, 1817–1862

NO ONE CAN SERVE TWO MASTERS; for either he will hate the one and love the other, or he will be devoted to the one and despise the other. You cannot serve God and mammon.

Jesus, Hebrew founder of Christianity, first century A.D. (Matthew 6:24)

Those who set out to serve both God and mammon soon discover that there is no God.

Logan Pearsall Smith, English writer, 1865–1946

Do not lay up for yourselves treasures on earth, where moth and rust consume and where thieves break in and steal, but lay up for yourselves treasures in heaven, where neither moth nor rust consumes and where thieves do not break in and steal. For where your treasure is, there will your heart be also.

Jesus, Hebrew founder of Christianity, first century A.D.
(Matthew 6:19–21)

And Jesus entered the temple of God and drove out all who sold and bought in the temple, and he overturned the tables of the moneychangers and the seats of those who sold pigeons. He said to them, **"IT IS WRITTEN, 'MY HOUSE SHALL BE CALLED A HOUSE OF PRAYER'; BUT YOU MAKE IT A DEN OF ROBBERS."**

Jesus, Hebrew founder of Christianity, first century A.D.
(Matthew 21:12–13)

THERE IS NOTHING new about poverty. What is new is that we now have the techniques and the resources to get rid of poverty. The real question is whether we have the will.

Martin Luther King Jr., U.S. clergyman and human rights leader, 1929–1968

THE GROWING DIVIDE BETWEEN WEALTH AND POVERTY, between opportunity and misery, is both a challenge to our compassion and a source of instability. We must confront it. . . . We cannot leave behind half of humanity as we seek a better future for ourselves. We cannot accept permanent poverty in a world of progress.

George W. Bush, contemporary U.S. president, 2002

The world is too much with us; late and soon,
Getting and spending, we lay waste our powers.

William Wordsworth, English poet, 1770–1850

If you live according to nature, you will never be poor; if you live according to public opinion, you will never be rich.

Epicurus, Greek philosopher, third century B.C.

THE GODS ARE THOSE WHO EITHER HAVE MONEY, OR DO NOT WANT IT.

Samuel Butler, English writer, 1835–1902

HE IS RICHEST WHO IS CONTENT WITH LEAST.

Socrates, Greek philosopher, fifth century B.C.

To be content with little is difficult; to be content with much, impossible.

Marie von Ebner-Eschenbach, Austrian writer, 1830–1916

We are poor not from what we need, but from what we want.

Josh Billings, U.S. writer and humorist, 1818–1885

ANNUAL income twenty pounds, annual expenditure nineteen nineteen six, result happiness. Annual income twenty pounds, annual expenditure twenty pounds ought and six, result misery.

Charles Dickens, English writer, 1812–1870

I am indeed rich, since my income is superior to my expense, and my expense is equal to my wishes.

Edward Gibbon, English historian, 1737–1794

He is rich or poor according to what he is, not according to what he has.

Henry Ward Beecher, U.S. clergyman, 1813–1887

Wealth is measured best not by what we have but by what we've given away.

Native American Proverb

OUR wealth is often a snare to ourselves, and always a temptation to others.

C. C. Colton, English clergyman, 1780–1832

Undefended wealth invites aggression.

Theodore Roosevelt, U.S. president, 1858–1919

Riches are gotten with pain, kept with care, and lost with grief.

English Proverb

Heavy purse, light heart; light purse, heavy heart.

English Proverb

Anyone who has ever struggled with poverty knows how extremely expensive it is to be poor.

James Baldwin, U.S. writer, 1924–1987

RICH in rubles, rich in sorrows; poor in rubles, richer in sorrows.

Russian Proverb

Much coin, much care.

English Proverb

Why is there so much month left at the end of the money?

Anonymous (U.S.)

There are people who can never forgive a beggar for their not having given him anything.

Karl Kraus, Austrian journalist and editor, 1874–1936

WATCHING WEARY SOULS
THE ONSLAUGHT OF POVERTY
TURNS THEIR EYES DOWNWARD.

Dennis Omowale Cutten, contemporary homeless man and poet

HE that is without money is a bird without wings.

English Proverb

Poor fowk are soon pish'd on.

English Proverb

ONE HUNDRED AND FIFTY SEVEN homeless people died on the streets of San Francisco this year and, as the nights get longer and colder, the situation is bound to get worse. Thousands are being turned away from shelters every night.

More and more people are being rousted while trying to find a safe place to sleep in parts or doorways; their meager belongings are confiscated and they are left with nowhere to go in this city that once prided itself on being humane and compassionate. We have gone, in the words of Father Kirk Ullery from Our Lady of Lourdes Catholic Church, "from the city that knows how, to the city that couldn't care less."

Lydia Gans, contemporary U.S. writer (January 1999)

Night after night, they die.
Night after terrible night
they sigh themselves away
in dumpsters, in burnt buildings,
in the back seats of junked cars
on the far edge of your cities.
They crowd your bedrooms in the dark,
they huddle under your silk sheets,
unseen, they bend over each sleeper
and touch with bloodied palms
this face, that breast,
given the task by a god
who wants no one to forget.

Peter Marin, contemporary U.S. writer, December 2000

IT IS VERY easy for rich people to preach the virtues of self-reliance to the poor.

Winston Churchill, British prime minister, 1874–1965

From poverty to wealth is a hard journey, but the way back is easy.

Japanese Proverb

Money is better than poverty, if only for financial reasons.

Woody Allen, contemporary U.S. writer, humorist, and director

The large print giveth, the small print taketh away.

U.S. Proverb

Counterfeit money is never lost.

Yiddish Proverb

It's not as good with money as it's bad without it.

Yiddish Proverb

IT doesn't matter if you're rich or poor, as long as you've got money.

Joe E. Lewis, U.S. comedian, 1902–1971

I've been poor and I've been rich. And believe me, rich is better.

Sophie Tucker, U.S. entertainer, 1884–1966

The lovers of money grow richer and richer, and the more they think of making a fortune the less they think of virtue; for when riches and virtue are placed together in the scales of the balance, the one always rises as the other falls.

Plato, Greek philosopher, fourth century B.C.

Wealthy men are insolent and arrogant; their possession of wealth affects their understanding; wealth becomes a sort of standard of value for everything else, and therefore they imagine there is nothing it cannot buy.

Aristotle, Greek philosopher, fourth century B.C.

THE INSOLENCE OF wealth will creep out.

Samuel Johnson, English writer and lexicographer, 1709–1784

To suppose, as we all suppose, that we could be rich and not behave as the rich behave, is like supposing that we could drink all day and keep absolutely sober.

Logan Pearsall Smith, English writer, 1865–1946

Poverty? Wealth? Seek neither—
One causes swollen heads,
The other, swollen bellies.

Kassiane, Byzantine nun and poet, 804–867 A.D.

WE may see the small value God has for riches by the people he gives them to.

Alexander Pope, English poet, 1688–1744

It is the wretchedness of being rich that you have to live with rich people.

Logan Pearsall Smith, English writer, 1865–1946

It is very difficult for the prosperous to be humble.

Jane Austen, English writer, 1775–1817

Probably the greatest harm done by vast wealth is the harm that we of moderate means do ourselves when we let the vices of envy and hatred enter deep into our own natures.

Theodore Roosevelt, U.S. president, 1858–1919

It must be great to be rich and let the other fellow keep up appearances.

Kin Hubbard, U.S. writer and humorist, 1868–1930

FEW of us can stand prosperity. Another man's, I mean.

Mark Twain, U.S. writer and humorist, 1835–1910

His money is twice tainted: 'taint yours and 'taint mine.

Mark Twain, U.S. writer and humorist, 1835–1910

UNDER EXISTING CIRCUMSTANCES wealth cannot be enjoyed without dishonor or forgone without misery.

George Bernard Shaw, British playwright, 1856–1950

Property has its duties as well as its rights.

Thomas Drummond, English engineer, 1797–1840

Surplus wealth is a sacred trust which its possessor is bound to administer in his lifetime for the good of the community.

Andrew Carnegie, Scottish-born U.S. industrialist, 1835–1919

Dirty hands make clean money.

Vermont Proverb

Better poor with honor than rich with shame.

U.S. Proverb

A SINGLE PENNY FAIRLY GOT
IS WORTH A THOUSAND THAT ARE NOT.

German Proverb

WEALTH, properly employed, is a blessing; and a man may lawfully endeavor to increase it by honest means.

Muhammad, Arab founder of Islam, 570–632 A.D.

Capital as such is not evil; it is its wrong use that is evil. Capital in some form or other will always be needed.

Mohandas K. Gandhi, Indian spiritual and nationalist leader, 1869–1948

No one would remember the Good Samaritan if he'd only had good intentions. He had money as well.

Margaret Thatcher, contemporary British prime minister

No wealth in the world can help humanity forward, even in the hands of the most devoted worker in this cause. Can anyone imagine Moses, Jesus, or Gandhi armed with the moneybags of Carnegie?

Albert Einstein, German-born U.S. physicist, 1879–1955

Business must be profitable if it is to continue to succeed, but the glory of business is to make it so successful that it may do things that are great chiefly because they ought to be done.

Charles M. Schwab, U.S. industrialist, 1862–1939

ONE rich man to two acquaintances at a men's club (cartoon caption): Money doesn't trickle down unless there's a damn leak.

William Hamilton, contemporary U.S. cartoonist

Money never made a man disgraceful yet, but men have often made money disgraceful.

Josh Billings, U.S. writer and humorist, 1818–1885

WOULDN'T YOU THINK some sociologist would have done a comparative study by now to prove, as I have always suspected, that there is a higher proportion of Undeserving Rich than Undeserving Poor?

Molly Ivins, contemporary U.S. journalist

The vices of the rich and great are mistaken for errors; and those of the poor and lowly, *for crimes.*

Countess of Blessington, Irish writer and salon host, 1789–1849

Ill fares the land, to hastening ills a prey,
Where wealth accumulates, and men decay.

Oliver Goldsmith, English writer, 1728–1774

If a free society cannot help the many who are poor, it cannot save the few who are rich.

John F. Kennedy, U.S. president, 1917–1963

THE WHOLE BUSINESS of the poor is to administer to the idleness, folly, and luxury of the rich; and that of the rich, in return, to find the best methods of confirming the slavery and increasing the burdens of the poor.

Edmund Burke, English statesman, 1729–1797

"AH, WHAT CAN I DO?" say a powerless few,
With a lump in your throat and a tear in your eye,
Can't you see that their poverty's profiting you?

Buffy Sainte-Marie, contemporary U.S. songwriter and singer

PEACE makes money, and money makes war.

French Proverb

When the rich wage war, it's the poor who die.

Jean-Paul Sartre, French philosopher, 1905–1980

The advantages of the rich over the poor cannot be maintained by anything but violence.

Leo Tolstoy, Russian writer, 1828–1910

Poverty is the worst form of violence.

Mohandas K. Gandhi, Indian spiritual and nationalist leader, 1869–1948

PROSPERITY CAN ONLY be lasting if it is based on justice.

Theodore Roosevelt, U.S. president, 1858–1919

Wherever wealth abounds, and the poor continue to suffer, we must confront God's judgment.

Mark O. Hatfield, contemporary Oregon senator

We'll all be richer when none of us is poor.

Harry Belafonte, contemporary U.S. singer, actor, and human rights activist

Money is like muck, no good except it be spread.

Francis Bacon, English philosopher, 1561–1616

To enjoy a good reputation, give publicly and steal privately.

Josh Billings, U.S. writer and humorist, 1818–1885

Soon gotten, soon spent; ill gotten, ill spent.

English Proverb

I KNOW OF NOTHING MORE DESPICABLE AND PATHETIC THAN a man who devotes all the hours of the waking day to the making of money for money's sake.

John D. Rockefeller Sr., U.S. industrialist, 1839–1937

Money is that dear thing which,
if you're not careful, you can
squander your whole life thinking of.

Mary Jo Slater, contemporary U.S. poet

The desire of acquiring the comforts of the world haunts the imagination of the poor, and the dread of losing them that of the rich.

Alexis de Tocqueville, French writer, 1805–1859

THE smell of money is sweet, whatever its source.

Juvenal, Roman poet, first century A.D.

Treasures gained by wickedness do not profit.

Hebrew Proverb (Proverbs 10:2)

THE rich are different only because people treat them as if they were.

Judith Krantz, contemporary U.S. writer

The only difference between the rich and other people is that the rich *have more money*.

Mary Colum, U.S. writer, 1885–1957

a louse i
used to know
told me that
millionaires and
bums tasted
about the same
to him

Don Marquis, U.S. writer and humorist, 1878–1937

The rich and the poor meet together; the Lord is the maker of them all.

Hebrew Proverb (Proverbs 22:2)

Read all three books in the series:

Inspiring Quotes

Love Quotes

Money Quotes